Spring

By Terri DeGezelle

Consultant:
Joseph M. Moran, Ph.D.
Meteorologist
Education Program
American Meteorological Society

Bridgestone Books
an imprint of Capstone Press
Mankato, Minnesota

Bridgestone Books are published by Capstone Press
151 Good Counsel Drive, P.O. Box 669, Mankato, Minnesota 56002
http://www.capstone-press.com

Library of Congress Cataloging-in-Publication Data
DeGezelle, Terri, 1955–
    Spring / by Terri DeGezelle.
    p. cm.—(Seasons)
    Includes bibliographical references and index.
    Contents: Spring—Spring temperatures—Water in spring—Trees in spring—Animals
in spring—People in spring—What causes spring?—Why do seasons change?—Seasons in
other places—Hands on: grow bean sprouts.
    ISBN 0-7368-1410-8 (hardcover)
    1. Spring—Juvenile literature. [1. Spring.] I. Title.
QB637.5 .D44 2003
508.2—dc21   2001008757

Summary: Explains why seasons change and describes the ways trees, animals, and people
    react to spring.

Editorial Credits
Christopher Harbo, editor; Karen Risch, product planning editor; Linda Clavel, designer
    and illustrator; Alta Schaffer, photo researcher

Photo Credits
Corbis, 21
Mark E. Gibson/The Image Finders, 14
PhotoDisc, Inc., cover (top left)
Richard Hamilton Smith, 20
RubberBall Productions, cover (bottom left)
Unicorn Stock Photos/Jay Foreman, 6; Tom McCarthy, 8; Paula J. Harrington, 12
Visuals Unlimited/Jim Whitmer, cover (main photo); Jerome Wexler, 4; Mark Gibson, 10

Artistic Effects
PhotoDisc, Inc.; RubberBall Productions

1 2 3 4 5 6 07 06 05 04 03 02

Table of Contents

Fun Fact

The first day of spring is called the vernal equinox (VUR-nuhl EE-kwuh-noks).

Spring

Spring is the season of new life. Flowers grow and animals give birth to young in spring. In the Northern Hemisphere, the first day of spring is March 20 or 21. Spring lasts three months.

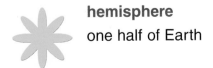

hemisphere
one half of Earth

5

Spring Temperatures

Temperatures outdoors start to rise in spring. The air begins to warm. Warm winds start to blow. The winds help melt snow and ice. People and animals enjoy the warm sunshine.

Water in Spring

Snow and ice from winter start to melt in the warm weather. Ice on lakes and streams begins to melt. Spring rains fall. The soil soaks up the water. The ground is ready for new plants to grow.

Fun Fact

Most apple blossoms are pink. Their color fades to white after they open.

Trees in Spring

Tree buds open into leaves during spring. Fruit trees grow flowers. The flowers change into fruit. Sap starts to flow inside tree trunks again. People tap maple trees to get maple sap. They make maple syrup from sap.

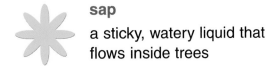

sap
a sticky, watery liquid that flows inside trees

Animals in Spring

In spring, bears come out from hibernation. They wake up from long winter naps. Birds return from the warm places they flew to in autumn. Birds start to make nests. They lay eggs in their nests. Sheep have lambs. Rabbits have bunnies.

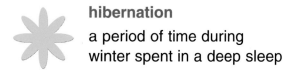

hibernation
a period of time during winter spent in a deep sleep

People in Spring

After a cold winter, people are ready to play outdoors. Baseball and soccer practices begin. Many cities and towns have festivals to celebrate the start of spring. Winter coats are put away. People carry umbrellas and wear raincoats on rainy days.

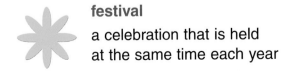

festival

a celebration that is held at the same time each year

15

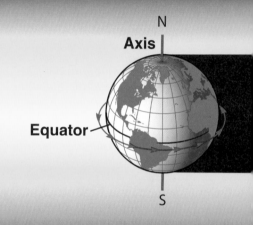

What Causes Spring?

Spring is caused by Earth's tilt. Earth spins like a top as it moves around the Sun. Earth spins on an axis. The axis is tilted. Spring begins when Earth's axis starts to point toward the Sun. On the first day of spring, the Sun's rays center on the equator.

axis

an imaginary line that runs through the middle of Earth from the North Pole to the South Pole

17

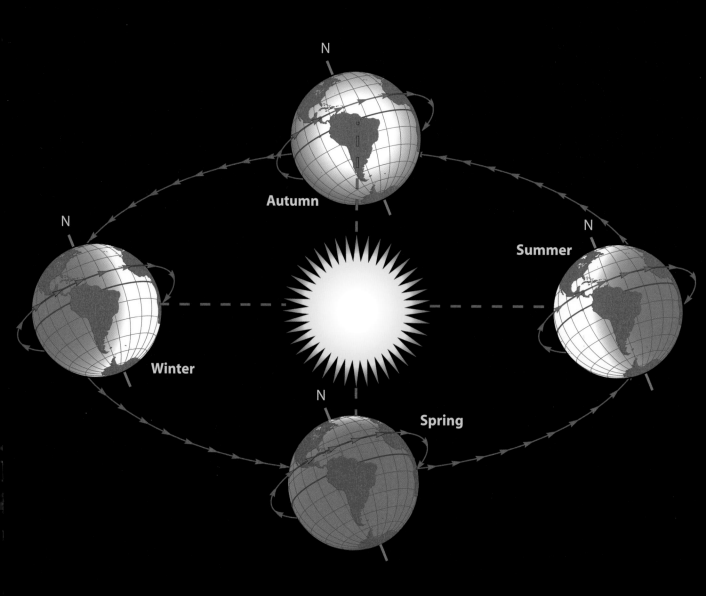

Why Do Seasons Change?

Earth makes one trip around the Sun each year. Earth's movement and tilt cause seasons to change. The Northern Hemisphere begins to lean toward the Sun in spring. The Sun is higher in the sky. Daylight lasts longer in spring than in winter.

When the Northern Hemisphere has spring, the Southern Hemisphere has autumn. Many farmers in the Northern Hemisphere plant their crops in March, April, and May.

At the same time of year, it is autumn in the Southern Hemisphere. Many farmers harvest their crops.

harvest
to collect or gather crops that are ripe

Hands On: Grow Bean Sprouts

Spring is the season of new life. In spring, people plant seeds in gardens and fields. You can see how a bean seed grows roots and a stem.

What You Need

Paper towel
Water
Clear plastic sandwich bag
Bean seed

What You Do

1. Soak one paper towel in water. Gently squeeze out any extra water.
2. Fold the towel in half and then in half again.
3. Place the wet towel in the plastic bag.
4. Place one bean seed in the center of the plastic bag.
5. Seal the top of the plastic bag shut.
6. Place the sealed bag in a sunny place.

In a few days, roots and a stem will grow out of the seed. Beans sprout this way in soil. The roots hold the bean plant in the ground and soak up water. The stem pushes itself out of the soil. In time, the stem grows leaves and beans.

Words to Know

axis (AK-siss)—an imaginary line that runs through the middle of Earth from the North Pole to the South Pole

equator (i-KWAY-tur)—an imaginary line halfway between the North Pole and the South Pole

harvest (HAR-vist)—to collect or gather crops that are ripe

hemisphere (HEM-uhss-fihr)—one half of Earth; the Northern Hemisphere is north of the equator.

hibernation (hye-bur-NAY-shuhn)—a period of time during winter spent in a deep sleep; some bears hibernate in dens.

season (SEE-zuhn)—one of four parts of the year; spring, summer, autumn, and winter are seasons.

tap (TAP)—to make a hole to draw out liquid; people tap maple trees to draw out sap for maple syrup.

tilt (TILT)—an angle to the left or right of center

Read More

Burton, Jane, and Kim Taylor. *The Nature and Science of Spring.* Exploring the Science of Nature. Milwaukee: Gareth Stevens, 1999.

Klingel, Cynthia, and Robert B. Noyed. *Spring.* Wonder Books. Chanhassen, Minn.: Child's World, 2001.

Stille, Darlene R. *Spring.* Simply Science. Minneapolis: Compass Point Books, 2001.

Internet Sites

BrainPop—Seasons
http://www.brainpop.com/science/weather/seasons/
index.weml
Maple Sugar in Nova Scotia
http://collections.ic.gc.ca/natural/maple/index.html
New Science—The First Day of Spring
http://kids.msfc.nasa.gov/news/2000/
news-vernalequinox.asp

Index